UNDER A PASSING SKY

Published by Kassala Publishing in 2011
Distribution peterwaine@rocketmail.com

Printed in Great Britain by the MPG Books Group, Bodmin
and King's Lynn.
Copyright © Peter Waine

Woodcuts by Thomas Bewick
Cover painting by Alan Tyers
Design by Oonagh Connolly at candc-design.com

ISBN 978-0-9563404-1-2

UNDER A PASSING SKY

Peter Waine

To hill and vale and distant view of rural England

TABLE OF CONTENTS

PART I

PART II

FOREWORD

Poetry is a hybrid friend. It is inordinately hard to write and it is very personal. To publish is akin to deep betrayal. Most of these poems were partly composed on country walks, a line or two comes instantly to mind and from nowhere. They need to be written down there and then or else they return to those same nether regions. Completing the stanza, however, can take weeks, even months and, alas, in some instances, never!

Part I is a tender celebration of England's rural idol. Part II is a reflection on the condition and experience of being human.

Peter Waine

Peter is National Chairman of CPRE (Campaign to Protect Rural England) and a former Chairman of both the Tree Council and The National Fruit Collection. He is also a former trustee of the Royal Opera House and member of ICC (International Cricket Council). He is a businessman and co-author or author of two business books and an acclaimed business novel. Peter has stood for Parliament and has been a Visiting Professor at both Warwick & Cass Business Schools.

PART I

THE RESTLESS SEA

What did you expect to see?
The east wind cuts, the tall reeds bend
The mud of the creek, the old marsh wall
And the square squat towers and bobbing masts
And the sad grey plover's call.

Little grebes dive and widgeons sleep
And the sky is awash on the wing
And the salt marsh stands by the restless sea
And a kindness of heart at the close of day
Transcends and settles on me.

BY ANCIENT RHYTHM

The year has turned, the ragwort heads the queue
The lower wood with snowdrops covered now
And strutting in the morning dew
The rook returns.

The capercaillie cuts the late spring air
And northern pinewoods sense its parting call
Whilst clustered cosy in the lair
The fox resides.

The lapwing flies by loch or upon fen
And piping redshank by the tidal wake
In kingly guard to watch the glen
The eagle soars.

At heaven's gate both thrush and blackbird sing
Whilst waxing moon will wonder through the night
The roosting bat will take to wing
The night unfolds.

THE BLACKTHORN STANDS

The blackthorn stands as Easter white
Its blossom falls with plum and pear
Together hold the peerless sight
And mantle all both far and near.

From vigil through to compline stand
The patient yew does clutch the hour
Whilst rusted plough the furrowed land
And resting suns will grace the tower.

SPECTRE

A splash of spring the canvas now conveys
By hedge and ditch and open fen displays
Beyond the poppied splendour tucked away
Wild rose, primrose, bell flower, wild mint and hay.
And rippled moss by crystal moving stream
Compounds, sustains the spirit's wildest dream.
The swifts return with summer in their wake
Their agile turns displayed by land and lake.
By deepest hush the welcome dusk descends
A chapter starts, another chapter ends.

SOON BY EVENING CALLING

By nature's brush with fetching hue
The bluebells paint the woodland blue
The sudden sound of pheasant cocks
The rhythm of the morning fox
Will stealthy mark the melting dew.

Where brambles climb and oaks preside
Once drover's way, now woodland ride
The leaning ash with hollow lea
A jumbled puzzle of a tree
Stands guard to nettles by its side.

Dull skylark gives the sweetest song
Sound of heaven than earth belong
With age the hedgerow takes its name
And choicest show of fare to claim
Where feasting eyes should linger long.

THE ASH

Without the ash, the sheep would roam
Without the hurdle gate no home
In foregone days, the harrow, plough and spade
By ash were made.

SEVERN SHORE

The starlings over Severn came
I could not count their score
They dived and dipped when on the wing
Against the Severn shore.

And gathered round were moon and stars
Sometimes distant thunder
How could I contemplate the view
There to watch and wonder.

WHERE IN WINTER

Where in winter stolen walks are made
On grassy banks and meadow fields
Butterflies in vibrant blue display
And rabbits play
Pure joy.

And dragonflies in tones of red
Or orange wings and patterned green
Land on path and fence and water's edge
Or sunny ledge
True joy.

THE UNINVITED

It comes and goes forgotten, the laurel's white caked flower
Unlike the bluebell where the woodland once had been
It never has its hour.

Where in peace – not poet's glebe – forsaken magpies fly
Unlike the favoured lark which echoes round the world
A dark allotted sky.

Foxgloves not by invitation gained yet stay as friend
In garden, dell and ditch and hollow by the stream
Till nearly summer's end.

THE DAFFODILS ARE DYING

The daffodils are dying
Their heads are hanging low
Speedwells in profusion
Break forth and overflow.

The rose in clusters hanging
Which one to pluck for you
The choice both hard and simple
Deep red or paler blue.

The sap no longer rises
And I no longer roam
So take my hand, but gently
And make the ground my home

A PERFECT DAY

As catkins paint the parting day
And bid the winter months away
While silver shade on sallow trees
And purple mist on northern breeze
With yellow hints on hazel trees
A perfect day to me.
And next to wait but not for long
The cuckoo's long departed song.
Then homeward thoughts of tea

LOVERS KISS

Before the white of elder flower
Becomes the nip of autumn fair
Between the sway of summer yield
On hedge and down, on fell and field
On lake and shore, on fen and heath
Lovers kiss and vow.

ENGLAND

When splash of red is mixed with heaven's gold
And lark ascends the patchwork view
In mellow fields the poppies stand
Before the silent dusk descends
The skylark reigns supreme.

Where spring comes soon and autumn waits at bay
And low stone walls by rising folds
Will paint the lane and boundless views
Then cattle pause by hawthorn's shade
The oak tree stands supreme.

The hedge of holly, ash and cherry fare
Portray the foxglove, swallow-herb
The hedgerow and the lanes combine
For lovers' time as those before
Harbours long the primrose flower.

NATURE'S SPREAD

A lovely sight the willow
The oak is lovelier still
The secret in the hollow
Is the wild daffodil.

The blossom in the home field
Lingers longer than the rest
The blossom in the orchid
Some will say is still the best.

The Norfolk Royal Russet
Or the Cornish Gilliflower
At anytime till sunset
Hanging heavy on the bower.

EVEN THIS

Oxslip stands in ancient wood
By the Mimram by the Lea
A cordant note of nature
Could its splendours be for me?

It maybe so, but linger
With coppiced ash my stool
Brief beauty of the mayflower dance
Above the fairest pool.

By step and dip and furrow
The country tells its tale
A little part of England
Green mantled by its vale.

The rooks they fly at Whitwell
Each tree is full in view
Yet I could part with even this
To pass my time with you.

THE EARTH GROWS OLD

The earth grows old
Yet young again by seasons new
Then bell by toll the steeple far
Will call the hare to break of day
And insects drone on summer hills
Each one by one the story told
Oh endless days yet cruelly few.

THE THISTLE

A week no more
Before the thistle blooms
And I to heaven be.
Ignored, passed by
Cut down and scorned
Yet all to me.

THE WIND IS STILL (VERSION 1)

The wind is still, the midnight hour
The frost, its labours done
Then dawn, late dawn, the darkness lifts
Far reach the distant sun.

The rutted field in winter
Is filled with waters new
But come the spring and bluebells
Then woodland touched in blue.

The sun depicts the mossy bank
A pallet splash of green
Whilst pines, in sun, in splendour
Complete the flawless scene.

From here the shepherd takes his flock
To mint encrusted hills
Through fields by busy woodland
Where brook and nature spills.

The lanes they share my secrets
Each walk a line or two
A pause for sad reflection
On this and that and you.

THE WIND IS STILL (VERSION 2)

The vacant wind, the midnight hour
The frost has laboured long
By dawn, the darkness lifts its veil
In time for chorus song.

Lifeless froze the rutted field
Yet hopeful is the scene
Bluebells soon appear again
To blue where brown had been.

The woods will home the mossy bank
The rising sun its feel
Beside the pines with wrinkled cloak
The longer days will heal.

From high on hill, to valley fall
The shepherd works the day
His knowing eyes the woodland take
To pass the hours away.

The heart will home my secrets all
One more as days are new
And sighs to hold my heart at bay
The many turned to few.

SUMMER'S LEASE

The summer lease is ending
The season's mottled hue
The squirrel's larder filling
A winter's moon in view.

Belonging to no season
In retrospect will rue
With outward signs of sorrow
And inward thoughts of you.

The distant rays of sunshine
Portray the parting view
The fields give way to ploughing
Before spring winds renew.

As dusk gives way to darkness
And trusted friends subdue
What once I felt uncommon
Is now just humdrum too.

HOMEWARD

The harvest safely home
And I to tea
By the fading wood
And aged yew, a special tree.

Below a passing sky
I know not where
Drover's way or lane
Will lead, by ancient track, nor care.

WONDERMENT

Stand, stand the oak at dawn
It grows in equal number
To the years of its decline.
Unnoticed near the lawn
The early purple orchid
And the open celandine.

But the lady smock
With its pretty little flower
Woos the cuckoo off its bower.

THE TURNING YEAR

The bracken brown in autumn rain
Where soon as shelter wren will find
A welcome home from winter's days.
Whilst on the bank, beside the ways
A woodland spread of narrow fronds
Yellow or green, upright or down
And brambles hide the woodcock well
Where gusty winds old branches fell.

ROBIN

Each note more perfect than the last
How can that be
Yet true I know
The robin on my apple tree.

BY THE RUSHES BY THE WATERS

By the rushes by the waters
The placid heron stands
Whilst nestled quietly in the lee
Beside the oldest apple tree
In tangled glade
And dappled shade
Is where the blackbird sings.

By tossing reeds and alder swamps
I heard the bittern boom
Before the gentle autumn tint
When leaves will boast their rustic glint
At close of day
The doughty jay
Conveys the acorn home.

EDEN

The spider spins and at first light
The thistle in its webbed delight.
Midwinter cannot dim for me
The glory of the oldest tree.

Lapwing tumbles by plough and wake
And coot with twig upon the lake,
While grass snake swims by reed and swamp
With little fanfare and less pomp.

The hedgerow in its glory now
From lowly dip to distant brow.
Four quarter moons the poppies bloom
By bridlepath and dreamlike comb.

The swallow caged by broken wing
No more the harbinger of spring.
The river flows from source to sea
Hurried, cautious and then it's free.

SEVENTH HEAVEN

When oxen ploughed the Western Weald
And snow lay in the parson's wake
And lark and owl did mark the hour
And honeysuckle paint the tower
Then Eden's gate was opened wide
And I did live before I died.

IN THE MENDIPS

I tell the truth!
The butterfly upon the thistle flower
Soon not one but many
And the moment soon an hour.

OCTOBER HAS ARRIVED

The leaves are golden, yellow now
Or pink or purple, float to ground
Till gusty winds ascend anew
And let me see again the view.
Cherry once red by berry, now by leaf
Others still bright red or dusty brown
October has arrived.

THERE IS A LOVELINESS

There is a loveliness that settles on this hour
When fading nettles join the yearly round
And robin red by autumn takes its turn
With martin, swift and swallow on the wing
And bending bowers where thrushes sing.

ON DAYS LIKE THESE

The heather pink and purple now
On vacant moor and open heath
Whilst harebells toll their fairy bells
On slender poles
And bees will sap the nectar fair
And swifts below an evening sky
Will twist as black then turn as bronze
On days like these.

LEAF AND BERRY

The fallen leaf
A token of the passing year
Near perfect, yet so brief
And soon to disappear.

A jewel unbound
Yet hanging long to be enjoyed
A berry crushed upon the ground
A work of art destroyed.

LOOK BY FORESHORE STANDING

Look by foreshore standing
Where waders linger long
With cliffs and hills surrounding
And eddies flowing strong.

Cows in cogent splendour
And swans parading by
The thistle dead and broken
And winter in the sky.

Thames with mist ascending
November days like these
The distant hills now mantled
Late rose upon the trees.

CLOSING DAYS

The hedge its moment comes again
With autumn mists and closing days
And berries red on naked twigs
As spindle leaves show pinker fair
With thorns against the greying skies
Stands long beside the bridleways.

PART II

THE KISSING GATE

The kissing gate so aptly named
When last I came this way
My luck was then to not foresee
In hopeless love, so helpless me.

It was a time of greatest joy
Youth and spring combining
But now the gate is broken down
And I am old and pining.

The bramble closes off the path
As time has quenched my joy
The gate now leads to emptiness
And time, my love destroy.

IT'S AUTUMN IN THE AYOTS

It's autumn in the Ayots
If it's spring in Mandalay
And winter in the tropics
If a year since hogmanay.

It means you are beside me
If my heart is all aglow
I care not then what season
Everywhere there's mistletoe.

THE FORTUNE TELLER

I listened to the fortune teller
All that I was told
I never found my four-leafed clover
Nor my pot of gold.

There are those who travel, some arrive
Which is it to be?
Cruelly felt the old year's fading light
At least it is to me.

Perhaps the fortune teller's clover
Was forget-me-not
Yes, yes I foolishly remembered
What even she forgot.

BRIEFLY

The spring of man and season
When hope outbids the two
When autumn seeks a reason
The answers will be few.

Beginning and an ending
Passing years, three score and ten
The dying leaves are falling
Not if, but rather when.

BY MOONLIGHT

Oh, let us meet by moonlight
My love, your hand in mine
By weir or folded hillside
Or humble celandine.

I caught the leaf when falling
And youth smiled back at me
From south the wind blew lightly
My spirit strangely free.

We walked the fields and byways
And laughed the distant view
But soon by evening calling
No lover's vow renew.

LIFE

Today is yesterday's tomorrow
Past joy can turn to present sorrow
Today's tomorrow's yesterday
What time gives, time too can take away.

So whichever way the dice is thrown
If a six, a four, a three or one
Or the two or even five is shown
You can finish only what's begun.

Some problems are square and some are round
Sometimes you're lost and sometimes you're found
Chances will come and chances will go
What you will reap is what you will sow.

MISTAKEN

Still I hear the lakeshore lapping
So beautiful and so nearly true
Yet even now the touch of autumn
Prepares me for an absent you.

Then something stirred across the field
And stirred within my heart
The afternoon of yesterday
Creates a broken heart.

The morning of tomorrow
Gives the soul a second chance
Yet tilting at the windmills
Constitutes a merry dance.

MUSING

April came, then May
And love was in their wake
What followed all too soon
Was sadness and heartache.

My dream, what dream
Countless times to naught
Better to have dreamed
Than not, or so I thought.

Which is worse? To know joy
And yet no more
Or never to have known
And be as mournful as before?

DONEGAL

I caught the wild wind
And the smell of the seaweed too
Donegal Bay was buried with foam
As I turned for home.

I wanted to be in Antrim for tea
Passing Wicklow on the way,
I walked through a wood home to nightingales
On the way to Bantry Bay.

I caught the scent of the summer wind
Heard the lonely curlew cry,
The buzzing of the passing bee,
Magic moments in July.

Alas, the boy became the man,
He did not choose this way,
Dawns did break and waves did break
From Mourne to Galloway.

HEARTLESS

Where beyond the far horizon
Will I next to seek in vain
Speak as if a wandering minstrel
Speak, but speak to spare the pain.

Conjured thoughts, departed weeping
Joyless stands the dawning day
My heart, no friend of mine by talking
Worthless words, like minstrel's play.

THE JOURNEY

Before the boy became the man
Or days all spent in life's full span
Magic was a summer scent
Hung upon the mountain air
Magic equalled love content
Like a wild unanswered prayer.

I wrote our names upon the sand
Before the coming tide
The tide came in, but you had gone
So what I wrote had lied.

You never saw my tear stained face
Against the autumn moon
Nor heard the undemanding words
Forgotten all too soon.

Those words unspoken by my lips
But spoken by my heart
Those words which wretchedly portrayed
Cast woefully apart.

And as the many years go by
I've often tried to reason why
Under a grey and leaden sky
Watching the embers slowly die.

LOVER TAKE MY HAND

Lover take my hand and walk the fields till noon
Cowslips standing proud with primrose now its June.
Where next? Our spirits wander far
Blessed by night, by solitude and star.

Time is tamed! The cosmos stands and by our love
The earth no longer spins, skylark sings above.
Then Dunster's clock will have its say
And weeping breaks the dawn's new day.

CARELESS TALK

So cruelly felt the winter wind
On hand and cheek and chin
But nil or little can compare
To what is felt within.

There was a moment brief in time
When hope imbalanced doom
And sanguine thoughts were uppermost
Before the endless gloom.

A TROUBLED DREAM

Even under a winter's sun
When all the summer's tasks are done
In the dark watches of the night
With harvest moon and strange half light.

Is there truth where truth does lie
When hopes and friends do falsify
Is the lover crushed in parting
At the end or at the starting?

Too much to ponder this for me
Constant conundrum, set me free
Oh, for lighter tones of laughter
Tomorrow and each thereafter.

GASTON AND SPENCER

I heard the cuckoo by Brocket Wood
And it filled my heart with joy
And beyond the wood the honeydew
Hence for long, so long I stood.

Without you now my spirit free
How silent is the day
Where over what your presence now
The Downs, the Weald, the sea?

IN THE SILENCE OF THE NIGHT

In the silence of the night
I heard Christ weeping
For his fractured world
Or did I dream whilst sleeping?

But then the rays of sunrise
Break the ice cold dawn
Robins raise their young
Stubborn hope engulfs the morn.

WHEN MY MOTHER DIED

Who will note my passing when I'm gone
Or mourn me as the losing of a friend
Will you note my absence with a sigh
Or will the lamentations be pretend?

For sure, I know of one who will be true
The curious wren in dextrous flight
Inclement weather, sunshine, light or dark
Equal friendship and to each delight.

PETER WAINE